Manage
the Media

Publisher's Note:
Memo to the CEO

Authored by leading experts and examining issues of special urgency, the books in the Memo to the CEO series are tailored for today's time-starved executives. Concise, focused, and solutions-oriented, each book explores a critical management challenge and offers authoritative counsel, provocative points of view, and practical insight.

Also available:

Climate Change: What's Your Business Strategy?
Andrew J. Hoffman, University of Michigan
John G. Woody, MMA Renewable Ventures

Five Future Strategies You Need Right Now
George Stalk, the Boston Consulting Group

High Performance with High Integrity
Ben Heineman, former General Counsel
of General Electric

Lessons From Private Equity Any Company Can Use
Orit Gadiesh and Hugh MacArthur,
Bain & Company, Inc.

MEMO TO THE CEO

Manage
the Media

(Don't Let the Media Manage You)

William J. Holstein

Harvard Business Press
Boston, Massachusetts

Library of Congress Cataloging-in-Publication Data is forthcoming.

ISBN: 978-1-4221-2148-1

The paper used in this publication meets the requirements of the American
National Standard for Permanence of Paper for Publications and Documents in
Libraries and Archives Z39.48-1992

Contents

How *Not* to Manage Relations with the Media

Chief executive officers are losing the battle for how Americans perceive them and the companies they lead. There's no clearer example than that of Robert Nardelli, the former CEO of Home Depot. Nardelli's $200 million–plus compensation package prompted an effort by organized labor to create a spectacle at Home Depot's 2006 annual shareholder meeting; in response, the CEO devised an abbreviated format for the meeting and cut off questioners, sparking a huge public relations disaster. Nardelli soon became "toxic," meaning that nearly all news media coverage of Home Depot revolved around the iron-fisted ways of an arrogant CEO. He was out of a job within a matter of months.

Other CEOs also have felt the sting of bad public relations—Hank McKinnell was hounded out of Pfizer, also because of a $200 million–plus retirement package (at the time Pfizer's stock had not appreciated significantly for some years). Lord Browne of BP, one of the most respected CEOs in the world, was drummed out. And Bill Ford at Ford Motor Company quit under pressure partly because he was never able to publicly articulate a convincing message about where the company was headed. In each case, there may have been an underlying business problem, but the attendant waves of negative publicity took on the force of unstoppable tsunamis.

The stakes are higher than just one figure's personal fate. The shellacking that companies receive, often over the issue of CEO compensation, knocks hundreds of millions of dollars off their market capitalization, which hurts executives, employees, and investors. And the negative environment also gives succor to activist shareholder groups, hedge funds, and private equity firms that may seek to force out CEOs and shake up boards. This climate can thwart many business objectives. Ultimately, the issue is, "Who's in charge of the corporation?"

It appears that the environment in which business leaders operate has undergone a structural change because of the proliferation of non-governmental organizations and other external groups and because of the burst of Internet-based communications that is taking place. "CEOs are losing the PR wars, and employees and the general public are losing their CEOs, which is not a good thing either," says Leslie Gaines-Ross, chief reputation strategist at Weber Shandwick, a public relations firm based in New York. "They're losing in some respects despite the fact that the economy is healthy and companies are innovating and creating new products that people want."[1]

I have been involved in covering major American companies for more than twenty years, as world editor at *BusinessWeek*, senior writer at *U.S. News & World Report*, and editor-at-large at *Business 2.0*. In recent years, I have specialized in covering CEOs and their boards as editor-in-chief of *Chief Executive* and *Directorship* magazines. In those capacities, I have interviewed dozens of CEOs and directors. Additionally, I have been able to study how CEOs see their businesses by writing a history of Cintas Corporation for Chairman Richard T. Farmer and by serving two years at American Express as a corporate writer. In that capacity, I had direct contact with James D. Robinson III, Sanford I. Weill, and Louis V. Gerstner Jr. So I have had many a ringside seat to battles between business leaders and the media.

The PR strategy, or absence thereof, was at the heart of what went wrong at Home Depot. In May 2006 Robert Nardelli was facing a concerted effort by the American Federation of State, County and Municipal Employees (AFSCME) to embarrass him at

Home Depot's annual shareholder meeting. A hard-hitting front-page story in the *New York Times* the day before the meeting relied heavily on information provided by AFSCME. The union's Richard Ferlauto, who was leading the attack, was astute in his ability to network with journalists and provide them with the kind of material they needed.

Nardelli decided to respond by discouraging his directors from attending the shareholder meeting and by imposing a tight limit on questions. According to my sources, Nardelli did not want to allow the union to "hijack" the meeting. Both internal and external public relations counsel tried to steer Nardelli from his dangerous course and warned him of backlash. But Nardelli ignored all PR counsel—and the media had a field day with the story, leaving Nardelli and Home Depot in a deep PR hole. The media did not report that there might have been a reason why Nardelli did what he did. All that Nardelli would say was that he had tried a new format for the meeting, but it didn't work and he would revert to a more open style the following year. To his credit, he did not assume a bunker mentality. He met with editorial boards for the *New York Times* and *Fortune*, among others. But his message fell flat—he apparently assumed he could ride out the negative coverage without being more forthcoming.

In the fall of 2006, I interviewed Nardelli for *Directorship* magazine, a small title aimed at a very high-level audience. I worked with top internal public relations representatives to set up a telephone interview. Then I conducted a thirty-minute interview with Nardelli. Our tone was cordial, but he refused to budge from his earlier statements and repeated the same formula to me over and over. He was clearly stonewalling. This is almost always a critical mistake.

When I prepared the transcript of the interview, I realized it was devastating. That had not been my intent; I wanted a fair account of what had happened. He might have had a credible message, if only he articulated it. I sent a copy of the transcript of the interview to Home Depot. This was an unusual journalistic practice, but it was so clear to me that it needed fixing.

Had Nardelli adjusted his answers and injected more credibility, he might not have been able to assuage all his critics but he might have demonstrated to at least some of them that there was a strategy behind his decision to run the shareholder meeting with an iron fist. But he chose not to.

The end result was an interview entitled "Nardelli's Mistake," which only compounded Nardelli's PR problem. The root cause appeared to be his conviction that, even though he was at the eye of an incredible

PR storm, that he could "gut it out," in the parlance of college football, which he had once played. It was of the last interviews he ever granted as CEO of Home Depot—he was forced out suddenly in early January 2007.

Ultimately, Relational Investors, a San Diego–based investment fund that owned only 1 percent of Home Depot shares, was able to use the Nardelli affair to push its own director onto the Home Depot board and secure the retirements of four directors who had been closely associated with Nardelli's pay package. "They won with 1 percent of the vote," Charles Elson, the governance expert from the University of Delaware told me. "It all goes to show that it's the message, not the messenger." This is an important point: if a company's opponents can define the message, they can win the day even if their raw economic power is relatively small.

Another company with a major public relations challenge has been Wal-Mart Stores. Looking back now, the key mistake that CEO Lee Scott made was that he allowed a loose Internet-linked network of unions; religious, community, small business, and equal-opportunity activists to coalesce into a force that could rally opposition to many different Wal-Mart initiatives. Critically, the company allowed its opposition to define what the issues were and to even define the very identity of Wal-Mart.

It seemed in the spring of 2006 that the company was encountering a "network effect" in which the forces of opposition were projecting far more strength together than they could have individually, a situation that was reminiscent of the antiwar movement of the late 1960s, when various activist causes—antiwar, pro-women, pro-minority—coalesced. In this case, Wal-Mart found itself in an almost purely defensive posture similar to that of the Nixon White House.

Part of the problem is that Wal-Mart had for years celebrated its small-town Bentonville, Arkansas, culture and values. That was helpful in penetrating rural America, but the company should have shifted gears earlier and become more culturally sophisticated. It also should have recognized that it could not simply stonewall the predominantly liberal New York–based media and the host of religious and labor groups that also had clear social agendas.

In the spring of 2006, I interviewed Paul Blank, who was campaign director of Wake-Up Wal-Mart, which is built around the Web site WakeUpWalMart.com. The key organizing force behind the Web site was the United Food and Commercial Workers International

Union, which obviously sought to unionize some Wal-Mart workers. It is one of two such union-backed organizations, the other being Wal-Mart Watch. Traditional methods of organizing workers simply weren't working. By developing a broader "movement," the union could project much more power.

At the time, the coalition claimed 235,000 members, including small business owners, environmentalists, and religious leaders. It was targeting Wal-Mart for its health-care policies and for allegedly allowing crime to fester in its stores, among other issues. "The 235,000 people are really representative of people of all walks of life," Blank said with almost evangelical zeal. "It is incredibly broad in terms of who has signed up."

Another, less likely, adversary was Sister Patricia Wolf, executive director of the New York–based Interfaith Center on Corporate Responsibility (ICCR) and a nun in the order of the Sisters of Charity, one of the 275 faith-based institutional investors that made up the broader ICCR. She and the Sisters of Charity had targeted Wal-Mart for what they regarded as Wal-Mart's poor track record in hiring and promoting women and minorities. The Sisters filed a shareholder resolution in seven different years, including every year since 2002. "The votes kept increasing," Sister Wolf said in an interview. "Last year, it reached 18 percent of the total. We thought that was a very good vote."

Wal-Mart, watching shareholder voting trends, gave in to the pressure and agreed to post its Equal Opportunity Employment data on its Web site, which henceforth would allow critics to measure its progress in hiring women and minorities. In the end, ignoring the nuns did not work.

The opposition has just kept growing. Roughly a year later, by the spring of 2007, the Wake-Up Wal-Mart group claims 366,085 members and proclaims on its Web site, "Join the most exciting, fastest growing social movement in America." And anyone searching for the words "Stop Wal-Mart" on Yahoo! got 10,300,000 hits (only 3,160,000 appeared on Google). There was some overlap among these sites. But however one counted it, it was clear that there were tens of thousands of sites dedicated to stopping Wal-Mart. One Web site featured a film from You Tube raking Wal-Mart over the coals for everything from racial discrimination in promoting minorities to environmental destruction to the destruction of small businesses. This was a grassroots brushfire.

In response, CEO Scott began demonstrating greater sensitivity to the coalitions of critics around him, but his recognition came late. Huge damage had been inflicted—and not just on Wal-Mart's image. There also were clear business and legislative consequences. The retailer has had trouble expanding into affluent Northeastern urban areas because of the negative perceptions it generated. Legislation was introduced in the state of Maryland mandating how Wal-Mart should treat its employees. An effort by Wal-Mart to expand into financial services ran into a political firestorm that forced it to relent. And the New York City Comptroller asked the U.S. Attorney General's office and the Securities and Exchange Commission to investigate Wal-Mart for "ill-considered and possibly illegal surveillance operations."[2] This was in connection with an internal "threat assessment" sleuth who monitored the communications of shareholders and critics.

Scott's effort to go on a charm offensive may have come too late. At the advice of a new team led by PR counsel Leslie A. Dach, he came to New York in late March to meet with the editorial boards of several major news organizations. But one of them, the *New York Times*, stung him with a headline, "Wal-Mart Chief Writes off New York." In his conversation with editors and reporters at the paper, Scott was asked about any plans to expand into the New York area, which had long resisted Wal-Mart. "I don't care if we are ever here," he was quoted as saying.[3] That was the wrong message.

The storm of negativity has become a self-fulfilling prophecy as more entrants seek to score off of Wal-

Mart's woes. Even Human Rights Watch, which normally concentrates on human rights issues in foreign countries, issued a report criticizing the way Wal-Mart has disrupted unionization attempts. A Wal-Mart spokesman said the company gave its employees "every opportunity to express their ideas, comments and concerns."

But the damage was done. A non-governmental organization dedicated to fighting for human rights around the world, and that therefore possesses a certain credibility, had attacked the giant retailer.

Even assuming that Wal-Mart is now employing the most sophisticated and best communications measures, it could take it years to recover the brand equity it had a decade ago.

One of the most remarkable displays of insensitivity from a CEO has been that of Countrywide Financial Corporation CEO Angelo Mozilo. He built Countrywide into the country's largest mortgage company in part by using creative financial techniques such as the "pay option" loan, in which borrowers choose how much they want to pay per month and add the rest to the loan's principal. It may work in the short term but it exposes the borrower to possible long-term trauma. Countrywide thus was at the epicenter of the subprime borrowing mess. The media were portraying the episode as one in which many lower-income Americans were going to lose their homes.

At the same time, it was disclosed that Mozilo had sold $140 million of his personal shares in the company in the past fourteen months, which was spectacularly bad timing. "If you're looking for a big winner in the subprime-mortgage meltdown, try Angelo Mozilo," *Wall Street Journal* columnist Alan Murray wrote in March. He concluded with this line: "As for Mr. Mozilo, he will emerge from the wreckage a very wealthy man."[4]

So Mozilo, at sixty-eight, has become toxic in much the same way that Nardelli did. Surely his public relations counsel, whether internal or external, should have spotted the unfolding irony and counseled Mozilo to make some sort of gesture to ease the appearance that he was cashing in on other people's misery. Few observers quarreled with Mozilo's right, at age sixty-eight, to reap some of the wealth he had created. But the "optics" were all wrong. And Mozilo attracted the attention of AFSCME's Ferlauto, which suggests there will be continued activism regarding Mozilo's compensation.

It's impossible to know statistically how many major CEOs have suffered because of poor media coverage, but it's clear that the phenomenon cuts across the

board in retailing, technology (think of Dell and Verizon), communications, and finance. "I think there are more losers than winners by far," says David F. D'Alessandro, former chairman and CEO of John Hancock Financial Services. "I think we're going to continue seeing more losers than winners."

What is the net impact? The eighth annual Trust Barometer study, conducted by Edelman Public Relations, showed that the credibility associated with CEOs declined from 28 percent of those individuals interviewed in 2006 to 22 percent in 2007. Even a regular employee of the company has greater credibility than that. "There is a divergence of opinion," says Richard Edelman, CEO of the firm that bears his name. "There is higher trust in business than ever before but trust in CEOs has declined."

It would be facile to say that executives simply have tin ears and are deaf to the steady drumbeat of negative coverage. But there are at least two major structural changes in how and why the media cover your companies—the first is related to the rise of shareholder coalitions and the second is the continued advance of Internet-based communications. These two trends appear to have caught many in top management by surprise.

Aside from NGOs, another new factor among activist coalitions is organized labor, which has been

steadily losing in the workplace for decades. But AFSCME, the AFL-CIO, the Carpenter's Union, and other major unions are creating or supporting the broad coalitions of critics, and they are creating an entirely new dynamic by targeting boards of directors, largely bypassing management. And they use the language of the shareholder because their own pension funds or those of various states, which include the funds of many union members, are major investors.

Labor leaders are adept at leaking or communicating the right information to newspaper reporters, who also are unionized in many cases. Like Ferlauto of AFSCME, a particularly skilled communicator is AFL-CIO Secretary-Treasurer Richard Trumka. He used his media savvy to target Verizon Communications CEO Ivan Seidenberg, whom Trumka says made $110 million over a five-year period. "I defy anybody to say this guy's earned the money," Trumka told the *Wall Street Journal*. He called Verizon "the poster child for pay for pulse"—meaning that the CEO was getting paid for simply being alive (i.e., having a pulse).[5]

In this particular encounter, Verizon was completely outgunned. Spokesman Peter Thonis said Trumka's "arguments are unfounded," but that language and logic were underwhelming. What Verizon did not say is that many of the options that make up

Seidenberg's package are "under water," meaning they are worthless unless the company's stock appreciates. So the figure that Trumka was using was in doubt. Nor was any mention made of the fact that Seidenberg is spending $18 billion of the company's money over a period of time to bring fiber optics connections to millions of homes. If it works, all Verizon's customers may benefit and the company could also reap huge new profits—Seidenberg could be a hero.

Another interesting twist of the AFL-CIO attack on Verizon is the pattern of alliances that the union sought out. The union, for example, approached Glass, Lewis & Co. and Institutional Shareholder Services (ISS). These firms rate the governance practices of companies and help shape the voting patterns of institutional shareholders sitting on trillions of dollars of equities. And the AFL-CIO said it would also meet with the office of the New York State comptroller and two of the nation's largest public pension plans—CalPERS and the California State Teachers' Retirement System.

The key to rallying these major allies was that Trumka has been able to articulate a message that resonated in the newspapers—and the company had not. No wonder that more than 50 percent of Verizon shareholders supported a proposal demanding an advisory vote on executive pay.

Adding to the toxic stew for companies vis à vis the media is the increasing prominence of academics, such as Lucian Bebchuk at Harvard, who are taking part in coalitions that attack CEOs and boards. The "movement" doesn't agree on every issue but can coalesce on certain issues, particularly CEO pay. So there has been a politicization of how companies are covered. "These groups are using tactics right out of Saul Alinsky's 1971 book, *Rules for Radicals*," says Dick Martin, chief of public relations at AT&T from 1997 to 2002 and now author of the book *Rebuilding Brand America*. "CEOs are in an election every day."

Aside from the proliferation of groups, another factor is technology, which has enabled this democratization effort. As per the example of Wal-Mart, blogs have reached the tipping point in terms of being able to generate news coverage in the pages of the *Wall Street Journal* and *New York Times* rather than vice versa. The blogs, as well as sites such as YouTube and MySpace, have intensified demands for immediacy and transparency that did not exist ten, or even five, years ago.

The vast majority of CEOs have not yet restructured their corporations and their various communications arms to respond to these new realities. In this environment, PR suddenly becomes something much bigger than PR. It becomes public diplomacy. It becomes corporate social responsibility. It becomes a vehicle that links employees in the pursuit of noble goals. It becomes the art and science of creating internal and external climates of opinion in which a company can achieve its objectives, not all of which are related to earnings per share. It is, in short, part of strategy.

In the climate that is rapidly emerging, coverage by all forms of media may be more important than ever because these channels reach all the constituencies that CEOs have to reach. Employees of a company attach far higher credence to outside media reports about their company than they do internal communications memos. Investors and analysts scrutinize media accounts carefully. Communities and customers also form crucial impressions from the media they consume.

The experts say it's a mistake for heads of companies to think they can end-run the media and communicate separately with the various constituencies. "Business has long understood the vertical (communications) axis, which is the top down," says Edelman. "They say, 'We'll speak to *BusinessWeek*. We'll speak to the financial analysts. We'll talk to Washington. And for the rest of it, we'll just do advertising.' But the model that now exists has a horizontal axis of communications. That is peer to peer and that includes employees talking to each other, MySpace pages, and blogs. All that is uncontrolled by the corporation."

To understand how CEOs might recover from their current dilemma, it may be helpful to understand how they got there. That's what the next section is all about.

What Went Wrong

Although some CEOs have done brilliant jobs in communicating and managing public perception (I'll describe them in subsequent sections), the vast majority have not.

The roots of the problem are deep. Most executives are not skilled at communicating with the media and don't enjoy it. They often have put the wrong people in place to manage the public relations function because they have difficulty in identifying the right set of skills. Furthermore, they have not structured their companies in such a way that they have the benefit of wise, ongoing PR counsel combined with timely, technologically savvy monitoring and response mechanisms. In such a vacuum, CEOs often needlessly compound the problem by turning to external PR counsel for advice without including their internal PR people. Instead of resulting in collaboration, this practice predictably creates a kind of trench warfare between internal and external PR resources. Even worse, CEOs sometimes turn to attorneys, whether internal or external, to devise and control communications strategies in crisis situations.

The root cause of the absence of PR savvy at the top is that boards don't normally place a high priority on communications skills when they hire a CEO, whether from within or from outside the company. In an exception to the rule, General Electric's Jack Welch contemplated communications skills when debating who should succeed him. Welch later told friends that one reason he and his board chose Jeff Immelt was that Immelt displayed a higher understanding of the need to communicate with multiple constituencies than did Robert Nardelli.

Nardelli was, and remains, a brilliant operational executive, as evidenced by his appointment as chief executive officer of Chrysler Corporation. He's known for an intensive focus on achieving results. But Welch was clearly right—Nardelli while at Home Depot had not risen to the level of an ambassador who could represent his brand in such complex times. Neither GE's nor Home Depot's stock has performed well in the past five years, but Immelt has been able to command the confidence of his board and the investment community, while Nardelli crashed and burned.

According to Spencer Stuart, the leading executive search firm, not a single CEO of a *Fortune* 500 company has had significant job experience in media or public relations. Among all major companies, the only exceptions to the rule may be Don Graham at the *Washington Post* and Peter Kann at Dow Jones, both of whom are former journalists.

The normal pattern is that CEOs work their way up the ladder through engineering, finance, sales, manufacturing, or other routes. The best CEOs today are those who have had years of experience in several of these siloes inside the corporation so that they can speak the language of the different warring tribes. But not communications. By the time leaders assume the corner office and encounter the intense pressures of being CEO, they tend to rely on instincts and core strengths. It's too late to learn a new discipline.

"How does a CEO become a CEO?" asks David D'Alessandro, head of John Hancock, who is highly unusual because he worked his way up through public relations and marketing. "Sometimes it's because they had the birthright—the proper silver spoon was inserted in their mouth. Most CEOs earn it by either coming straight up the organization, working twenty-five years, which is in and of itself its only little culture, unlike a culture across the street. They're very isolated in many ways. They're in their own world. Then of course, you have the gunslingers who move around."

"In each case, a cocoon is being spun around the CEO and that creates royalty," he adds. "It gets to a point that, despite how smart many of these people are, that cocoon actually makes them believe that the rules are different for them."

CEOs have usually been in environments they have been able to control, so being exposed to the media's crossfire is discomfiting. "They don't understand the press at all," D'Alessandro argues. "They actually think the press acts like a business where the publisher of the *New York Times* walks into the business newsroom and says, "Hey, this guy Bernie Ebbers is a good guy. He gave $2 million to something. I want you guys to lay off.' These guys do not understand the First Amendment. They don't understand how it works and they do not believe it applies to them."

Not surprisingly, many chief executives I've met or interviewed over the years have had a negative bundle of attitudes toward the public relations profession. One strand of thinking is that PR is a "soft" endeavor. There's relatively little that can be quantified and documented about the success of a public relations team, which raises suspicion in the minds of CEOs who like to possess hard data. You don't respect something that can't be measured.

It's true that CEOs have access to very sophisticated tools such as favorability studies from the likes of Nielsen Media Research, Roper, and Gallup to measure the public's attitudes toward their company. These indicators include brand and reputational issues, and a company's advertising may play an important role in shaping those perceptions. But it is usually quite difficult to document how a public relations strategy has had a direct impact on reputation numbers. It's even more difficult to quantify the impact of solid communications on a company's share price. The vast majority of PR people insist there is a correlation, but they simply can't prove it.

Another misperception that chief executives often have is that their public relations team ought to be able to control what the media write or broadcast. This is a breathtakingly naive view, because the American media, by definition, is much more independent than the media of any other country. Journalists pride themselves on not being controlled or even influenced by the companies they cover. Yet I've heard CEOs say, "Just PR it." The implication is that PR people possess a black box of tricks that they can play to guarantee positive coverage. That's entirely unrealistic, yet when there is a negative story, it is considered a PR "failure."

And although virtually all CEOs care deeply about their companies' brand name and reputation, you have a very defensive posture when it comes to engaging with the media. When I once asked for an interview, the CEO of a major consumer products company told me, "I'll just let my numbers do the talking for me. The minute I come out and say something, I just invite attack."

It's true that the media are skeptical. With the notable exception of the late 1990s when executives were lionized by an adoring press, the media have been all too ready to take corporate leaders to task. In his 2005 book, *Tough Calls: AT&T and the Hard Lessons Learned from the Telecom Wars*, former PR man Dick Martin tells of how in January 1996 AT&T CEO Robert Allen announced the layoff of forty thousand employees as part of a major restructuring, setting off a wave of negative coverage. The *New York Times* dubbed Allen a symbol of "corporate avarice."

Martin wrote that internal PR people recognized that the company was playing with fire and sought some small symbolic gesture. They argued, for example, that executives and directors should donate some of their salaries and fees to a fund for fired employees. They were ignored.

The problem became much worse when the company disclosed within a matter of weeks that the board had granted Allen a special 1995 stock grant worth $9.7 million. He appeared to have profited personally by firing forty-thousand people. Not surprisingly, the media coverage became even worse. A February 26, 1996 *Newsweek* cover story proclaimed Allen a "Corporate Killer."

The cynical, insensitive nature of accepting a large personal financial gain at the same time that other AT&T employees were suffering had completely escaped Allen, his top management team, and his board. "We thought it was a disaster and we should do something about it, but he was getting all his advice from the CEO club," meaning other company heads around the country, Martin recalls in a recent conversation. "He wasn't going to listen to his PR people when he had Jack Welch telling him, 'Hang in there. Remember what the media used to say about me being Neutron Jack.'"

When CEOs do choose to engage with the media these days, Martin says they sometimes try to do it incorrectly by attempting to mimic the model that the White House uses. "They look at how President Bush handles the press," says Martin. "They say, 'We'll stonewall them. We'll only talk to the ones who are friendly. Or we will go around the national press and go straight to the local media.'" In Martin's view, that approach is "a nail in the coffin" because it falls short of the more genuine, robust engagement he advocates and because it risks media backlash.

Of course, one reason chief executives haven't trusted their own PR people in many cases is that the skills sets and background of too many communications professionals have not kept pace with changing times. Although there are clearly exceptions, the reality is that a certain percentage of those involved in communications functions have traditionally been people who have not been successful in other careers at their companies. "Corporate communications was a dumping ground for people who weren't succeeding at the company, or it was a sunset position as they transitioned out. The tone was often, 'How bad can they screw it up?'" says George H. Jamison III, head of the communications search practice for Spencer Stuart and former head of communications at United Technologies Corporation and Hughes Electronics.

In Jamison's view, PR personnel understand how to write press releases and newsletters, how to manage a corporate Web site, and how to arrange interviews and background briefing sessions. But they lack deep understandings of the company's business and how global and technological trends—the issues that keep CEOs awake at night—will affect the company.

"In the talent pool, what you run into is many people who haven't broadened themselves to fulfill these roles," Jamison says. "They have a very traditional definition of media relations.

"What is required is a very thorough and savvy understanding of how the business works and what the market forces are and what the technological and political forces are," he adds. Unless they possess that dimension, "they are not in position to be the kind of adviser they ought to be. They don't have the intellectual horsepower to sit at the table with senior management and talk about the future of the company."

The end result can be a mutually reinforcing downward cycle. Leading executives have a basic disposition to mistrust PR people, and PR people tend not to understand business issues. As a result, PR's function is not viewed as being an important contributor to the company's overall success.

Consequently, CEOs do not tend to structure their reporting lines in a way that the top communications person, often a senior vice president, reports directly to them. "The very toughest part of the job is getting a seat at the table," says Martin. "Then you have to become an ally. You can't be perceived of as a threat by the CFO and general counsel or anybody else at that table. They're worried that you're going behind their backs to talk to the CEO. It's a politically difficult job."

Internal PR people often report to a corporate counsel, chief financial officer, chief marketing officer, or even a human resources executive. Typically, these executives either block direct communication between top PR staff and the CEO or else filter the message. Lawyers in particular seek communications strategies that put an emphasis on stonewalling and silence. That may be legally sound, but it's disastrous from a PR perspective.

If the top communications executive is not at the table where the top team makes decisions, the communications dimension of asking, "How is this going to sound to the outside world?" or "Is this statement going to withstand media scrutiny?" is absent. The CEO makes a decision that is then communicated, again through a management layer, to the PR shop. "In too many cases, PR people are out of touch and don't know what's going on," Martin says. "They are simply told what to say"—which means they may have the unpleasant, and ultimately doomed, task of communicating a poorly formulated message.

Another structural issue is the bifurcation of communications functions between public relations and investor relations (IR). Almost never does the IR function report to the senior vice president of corporate communications. IR professionals typically report to a treasurer or chief financial officer, which makes a certain amount of sense, particularly in the Sarbanes-Oxley era in which CEOs and CFOs can go to jail if there is a misrepresentation of financial results.

But it makes no sense if there is no coordination, which is typically the case. IR specialists see their job as communicating exclusively with Wall Street analysts and institutional investors. "The IR people would rather die a thousand deaths than talk to a reporter or even the public relations people at their own company," says James Horton, a principal at New York–based PR agency Robert Marston and Associates.

Yet there is a joined-at-the-hip relationship between analysts and journalists. The reporters need analysts to quote for their stories and the analysts need to be quoted to communicate their points of view about a company as forcefully as possible. Because analysts and journalists talk to each other a great deal, they may notice that a CEO's message is disjointed because PR practitioners are presenting it in one way and IR practitioners in another. That creates distrust and misunderstanding, which is precisely the opposite of what a CEO should be attempting to achieve.

One last element of organizational challenge is the use of external PR counsel. There are some very solid, seasoned external PR counselors who can offer sound advice to the chief executive. They also can do things that internal staff cannot do; for one thing, these firms can develop and maintain relationships with editors, reporters, and producers far more easily than, say, internal PR staff based in Peoria, Illinois (Caterpillar), or Atlanta (Coca-Cola).

Those relationships are absolutely essential. Despite all the expressions of hostility between the PR profession and the media, the two depend on each other in a kind of symbiosis. The best PR people know key journalists on a first-name basis and support their professional organizations or see them socially. Journalists, in turn, rely on smart PR people for ideas and for access to top business leaders.

But many of the larger PR firms, particularly those now owned by advertising agencies, concentrate on winning the big corporate account and then turn it over to legions of twenty-somethings who proceed to call journalists to update their databases of media contacts when, in fact, journalists don't want to be in anyone's database; and they don't want a steady blitz of e-mails, phone calls, or "snail mail." In fact, many top journalists have devised a system specifically to screen out the clutter from PR firms. They don't monitor or respond to the phone numbers and e-mails on their business cards—their real phone numbers and e-mail addresses are known to a far more limited circle.

Mass PR strategies may be quantifiable ("We sent out ten thousand e-mails and made twenty thousand phone calls.") and therefore warm the heart of a business client. But they hardly represent a sophisticated media outreach program. In fact, they may inflict damage on a company's reputation.

Even if you have the good fortune of identifying a sophisticated outside PR firm, relations between external PR counsel and internal PR professions are typically quite contentious. They are engaged in a battle for credibility in the eyes of the CEO. I once was offering informal counsel to a very senior New York–based public relations professional for a major European company that had taken a hit in the headlines. This executive had scheduled an editorial board meeting for his CEO with the editors of the *Wall Street Journal*.

But his external PR firm created a major flap, arguing that the meeting should be cancelled because of the risk that the editors would ask hostile questions. To my journalistic eye, canceling the session would have been suicidal because it would have solidified the suspicion in the minds of the *Journal* editors that the chief executive had done something wrong, or had knowledge about someone else who did something wrong. If would be far better to take a few tough questions, and politely deflect them, than to cancel.

The internal PR professional prevailed in this battle, and the meeting did occur. But why would an external PR firm openly confront a seasoned internal PR team? "Because it wasn't their idea," says the internal executive. In other words, there is often a political battle between internal and external PR forces, particularly when a CEO is directly involved. That is compounded in complexity if you are using multiple external PR firms.

In my experience, most senior executives don't fully understand the tangle of issues bedeviling their communications strategy. They tolerate a measure of dysfunctionality during "routine" periods and largely seek to remain disengaged. But in times of crisis, they tend to plunge in. Once a company is locked in a PR crisis, however, particularly in today's superheated environment, the risks of making PR blunders are huge.

In crisis situations, lawyers tend to dominate the decision making. That means saying as little as possible. Internal PR representatives rarely have the clout that a general counsel does or even an external legal adviser. Robert Marston, head of Robert Marston and Associates, says he has witnessed many battles over whether a company should be candid and forth-coming in its communications. Internal PR people made the case for candor. But in one case, a white-haired lawyer from a major law firm told the CEO and top management, "You can do this, but be ready to go to jail." Faced with statements like that, most CEOs take the careful approach recommended by lawyers.

David D'Alessandro tells a particularly revealing story about a crisis that occurred while he was CEO at John Hancock. The company faced a class action lawsuit worth billions of dollars for "switching policies" on its customers, which meant (1) it increased the value of customers' policies without notification so that the customers suddenly owed more money or (2) it sold policies based on continued stock market gains, so that when the market headed down, policyhold-ers also suddenly owed more money to Hancock.

At a board meeting, D'Alessandro's attorneys sug-gested he fight the suit. "They believed you could fight an immoral act by delaying the consequences through a long-drawn-out, expensive legal battle. They thought they were the smartest guys in the room. They were going to make a ton of money whether we won or lost. They did not care about our public relations prob-lem. They said, 'Just shut up.'

"Meanwhile, the press was looking for human condition stories—the woman who lost her house

nsurance payments blew up. The pub-
med because it turned out there were
tens of thousands of these people. As I sat in a room,
I listened to the public relations people and I listened
to the lawyers. I asked a simple question, 'Did we indeed steal from these people?'" The lawyers asked
him to define *stealing*, which he did. They said, "Well,
if that's your definition of stealing, then we stole."
The lawyers continued to argue that they should
spend $80 million over a seven-year period to fight
the case.

"But how much of a reputational hit would we
take in that seven years?" D'Alessandro recalls won-
dering. "The answer is immeasurable because you're
still trying to sell stuff. And how can you sell stuff if
you're getting sued for stealing?" D'Alessandro decided to settle the case for $750 million, disregarding
the advice of his lawyers.

Because so many competing voices are heard, chief
executives are often trapped in a highly dysfunctional
and defensive PR environment at the very moment
that the voices attacking them are extremely sophisticated in using the media to their advantage. Your
internal PR people often live in a state of fear and
paranoia because their own top managements expect
them to "control" the media, when in fact the media

cannot be controlled. The media, in turn, expect PR representatives to make top executives available for comment, when in fact the PR people may lack the credibility to persuade their top executives to do it.

Internal PR people manifest their aversion to risk in other ways as well: many PR people rarely answer their telephones and have recordings saying, "If I'm not available, call so-and-so." Infuriatingly, that person is also not available. So journalists often have great difficulty in getting PR people to talk to them, which is presumably core to their job descriptions.

One reason journalists find it difficult to get through to the right PR people is that most public relations shops are woefully underfunded and therefore lack adequate numbers of people. It's no surprise that if you attach scant value to the PR function, you would not allocate large sums of capital to it.

But the net result is that PR people are overwhelmed by all the calls from the media and have to engage in a kind of triage operation when deciding to whom they will respond and to whom they won't. Obviously, journalists who don't get responses or who have to badger PR representatives become angry, and that, in turn, affects their coverage.

All of which is in sharp contrast with the activist groups or investors or law firms that may be attacking a company. In those cases, principal players are responsive in real time and are adept at "spinning" the story. They understand the importance of the media and place great emphasis on communicating their message. Journalists on deadline are likely to feel much more warmly toward a source who returns calls promptly and has a handle on the subject matter.

If in contrast, a corporation has a muddled message, and its communications functions are riven with internecine rivalries, and if PR functionaries can only say "no comment," the opposition will be able to define the story. For all these reasons, too many CEOs are simply outmaneuvered and outgunned.

Incorporate Communications
into Corporate Strategy

One of the characteristics that makes American capitalism so flexible is that chief executives respond to different challenges as they arise by changing the structure of their companies and by shifting resources to meet the next generation of demands. There was once a "quality" movement, for example. At first, companies created quality departments but then realized that they needed to integrate a commitment to quality into every aspect of how their companies operated.

There was also a "reengineering" movement to encourage senior leaders to reevaluate pieces of their business that were no longer competitive or had somehow grown fat and soft. Today, CEOs and their top management teams are constantly reengineering businesses by shifting operations to India or China, for example. There is a massive reshuffling of corporate functions under way. But the buzzword "reengineering" has largely disappeared from the lexicon.

Similarly, in response to the rapid emergence of coalitions of critics, shareholders, and investors, and in recognition of the increasing prevalence of Internet-based communications, there appears to be a growing consensus among thought leaders today that the broad role of communications must be more deeply integrated into how CEOs chart their business strategy. Communications can no longer be a sideshow. "The best strategy is where PR has broad reach and deals with anything that can affect corporate reputation," says Robert Marston. It should be "a critical function in management's quest to attain their business objectives," adds George Jamison.

That suggests that U.S. companies, from the board level on down, will increasingly need to build communications concerns into their very DNA. Boards will need to evaluate a CEO's communications style and effectiveness. You will have to recognize that you personally must be involved in addressing shareholders through the media. You will have to select senior public relations counsel and public affairs advisers whom you respect and structure their organizations in such a way that these functions have real clout. There are specific strategies and tactics that I will discuss in subsequent sections, but the first step is getting the basics right.

For boards, the challenge is to manage the CEO succession process over the long term by taking into consideration the skills and the values of the pool of candidates. Boards are not currently well equipped to do that because they themselves lack expertise in public relations, but it's a challenge they can no longer shirk. CEOs, lead directors, and heads of nominating committees have consciously sought to shape board membership to address challenges in technology, finance, governance, globalization, and other crucial areas. Why should boards not also place a premium on communications and incorporate at least one director with relevant experience?

If boards incorporated a sensitivity to public relations, they would then understand more about how to groom CEOs who also are adept at communicating a company's core messages. They would recognize that candidates for CEO and other "high-potential" leaders should have the benefit of media training and be exposed to media interviews on their way up the corporate ladder so that they are trained and seasoned.

It's not out of the realm of rationality to suggest that some high-potential candidates obtain direct experience in managing communications functions. In today's prevailing climate, however, if an executive on the fast track were to be told to report for duty in corporate communications, it would be seen as a clear demotion—it would send the signal that something has gone awry. But it shouldn't. A communications assignment should be part and parcel of any CEO aspirant's training.

CEO candidates should also display the right communications values. One litmus test for any candidate should be whether he or she understands and embraces what is known in the trade as "the *New York Times* rule," which is to ask: "If I make a certain decision, how would it look if it appeared on the front page of the *New York Times*?"

In my experience, one CEO who best embraced this ethos is Fred Smith, founder and still CEO of FedEx. I saw how Smith built the rule into his thinking at a judging session I organized in early 2006 while editor-in-chief of *Chief Executive* magazine. The judges had gathered to select the magazine's next CEO of the Year. Judges included Smith; Maurice R. "Hank" Greenberg, former CEO of AIG; George David, CEO of United Technologies (the outgoing CEO of the Year); and Charles Lee, former co-chairman of Verizon Communications and a member of the board of Procter & Gamble.

After the conclusion of the judging session, which resulted in the selection of A. G. Lafley of P&G, Lee offered to send samples of the latest Gillette razor product to each judge. P&G had acquired Gillette and was in the process of integrating it. "Boy, how would this look in the newspaper?" Smith quipped. He could see the headline: "Corporate Titans Get Free Razors." Even worse would have been: "Titans Name Laffley, Get Free Razors."

It was all in jest, and the razors had absolutely nothing to do with the decision making, but Smith's comment reflected a very strong communications sensitivity. Smith obviously conducts his business and his professional life with a keen sense of how it would appear to the public. That's part of the sensibility that board members should seek in selecting a CEO.

Once in place, a chief executive needs to make communications a priority. It doesn't need to take up 10 percent of a CEO's time, but it has to be more than 0 percent. E. Neville Isdell, chairman and CEO of The Coca-Cola Company, addressed this need in a widely noted interview at the World Economic Forum annual meeting in early 2007. Asked about escalating demands for "accountability" and "transparency" from activist shareholders and others, he said: "Corporate leaders face a critical choice: to engage these stakeholders or turn a deaf ear, to complain of unfair treatment or accept the fact that accountability is part of the social license to do business."[6]

Isdell is obviously one CEO who has recognized the changing environment. CEOs like him who "get it" develop clarity of expression and use plain English in all external communications. And they understand that the CEO's personal involvement in media relations is essential. No one can remain in the bunker. "What happened in the wake of Enron and Tyco," says Richard Edelman, "was that many CEOs said, 'The way to succeed is keep your head down and make your numbers.'

"But in the past year or two, you can see some CEOs have recognized that is not a success strategy," he adds. "They see that, in fact, there are other stakeholders out there beyond Wall Street that you have to satisfy. Whether it's Wal-Mart or General Electric, smart CEOs are stepping out and saying, 'I want to talk to the green movement. I want to talk to our local communities. And I want to talk a lot to the employees.' I think increasingly CEOs are recognizing that a major part of their responsibility is communicating to employees and customers. All this is absolutely central to the success of their tenure."

One way to reach all those constituencies at once is through the media, and only the CEO's voice and personality will cut through the communications clutter. Business reporters, the vast majority of whom have never worked inside a nonmedia company, do not truly understand what CEOs do for a living and often form judgments about companies on the basis of a CEO's personality. That's one problem Ford had— Bill Ford simply refused to speak with reporters in the vast majority of cases. That created a kind of cat-and-mouse game—the journalists who did obtain infrequent access to Ford tried to catch him in a misstatement or draw him into subject areas such as yoga or the environment where he would appear confused. It was disastrous for Ford—both the man and the company.

In sharp contrast, Ford's new CEO Alan Mulally has an engaging personal style that is a winner with the media. Even with his company facing its darkest moments in many years, Mulally staged a tour de force by appearing before a massive gathering of automotive journalists at the 2007 New York International Auto Show.

Most CEOs would wake up in a cold sweat if they contemplated appearing before hundreds of journalists without prepared remarks and simply responding to questions. But that's what Mulally did, in a remarkable display of sangfroid and confidence. And he knew how to employ humor. He told a story about meeting President Bush at the White House to unveil a hybrid automobile and then gushed, "This is off the record, isn't it?" That produced guffaws.

Then he paid homage to Toyota executives in the audience and said, "This is friendly competition." Which, of course, it is not. The fact that Toyota is engaged in a full-fledged effort to bury Ford and General Motors made Mulally's ironic comment another hit with reporters.

So Mulally is reaping dividends with the media because of his personal communications style. The prevailing tone of coverage toward Ford Motor has shifted from calling it a failed company toward calling it a company in transition. It may be difficult to believe, but Mulally's communications skills could help determine whether he has sufficient time to complete the company's turnaround efforts.

Once the right CEO with the right skills is in place, the next step is to select a top communications counselor. It is easy to get blindsided by an issue, particularly if it is social or political in nature. Yet CEOs accustomed to the realms of finance or technology often do not know how to evaluate the skills of PR people.

The key is choosing someone on the basis of seniority and experience, rather than for interpersonal style, which seems to have been one key distinguishing criterion in the past. Another trap I have seen CEOs fall into is choosing a top communications person who merely "gets ink" for the boss, but doesn't focus on helping the whole institution communicate a winning message. It may be gratifying, egotistically speaking, in the short term, but it's not a winning strategy for the long haul.

Spencer Stuart's George Jamison says CEOs should look for someone who can be a *consigliere*, the Italian term for adviser or counselor. The term was made popular through Mario Puzo's *Godfather* movies. The consigliere was a senior, trusted, nonpolitical adviser who would whisper the truth to Don Corleone.

Dick Martin says smart CEOs will identify a counselor who has much broader skills sets than simple media relations. "What a CEO is looking for is judgment about business problems, creativity in solving those problems, and integrity, which is being willing to tell the CEO he's wrong," the former AT&T executive says.

It's not at all clear that former journalists should be in charge of a company's PR strategy. We may have keen communications skills and a deeply intuitive understanding of how the media operates, but we tend to lack management experience and not to have as deep an understanding of strategy as the CEO does.

That seems to be key—the top communications person has to understand the business through the CEO's eyes. One such senior vice president who has won accolades recently for being able to do that is Steve Harris, who came out of retirement to take over communications functions for General Motors CEO Rick Wagoner. Harris has direct access to Wagoner and was instrumental in crafting a communications strategy that helped fend off both billionaire investor Kirk Kerkorian and Nissan-Renault CEO Carlos Ghosn.

The portfolios of these top communications professionals should reflect their stature. There is no single method of organizing the communications functions that is superior to all others. But the appointment of Tom Mattia as senior vice president of Worldwide Public Affairs and Communications at Coca-Cola in January 2007 was an example of one successful strategy. First, Mattia reports directly to CEO Isdell. Second, he is a veteran—with thirty-five years of wide-ranging experience at Ford, Electronic Data Systems (EDS), and IBM—and has worked in brand management, media relations, advertising, and online marketing, among other areas. Third, he has joined the company's executive committee, which is where many critical decisions are made. And his position includes these functions:

- Corporate communications

- Public policy

- Employee communications

- Archive functions

- Corporate responsibility

- Both the company's Public Policy and Corporate Responsibility Council, and the Bottler Public Affairs Advisory Board

That's a very similar portfolio to what his predecessor had, but it's an example of how some smart CEOs structure the job so that it has clout. Mattia's position, experience, and portfolio send a clear signal to the rest of senior management that he is a force to be reckoned with. It's noteworthy that Isdell relies on committees to help knit together various functions such as marketing, governmental affairs, and corporate social responsibility. Each may have separate reporting lines, but they are forced to coordinate their efforts.

But that's not the only way to organize the strategic PR function. David D'Alessandro organized his communications functions at John Hancock slightly differently. It didn't spare him from getting into hot water with the class action lawsuit, but it was nonetheless a sound strategy. He recommends it to today's CEOs: "I would have a PR department that consisted of top-line business journalists and lawyers," he explains.

"They were not the same people who produced product publicity or the normal press releases. They were my own private watchdog group that worried about anything in the company that could potentially blow into a major problem. They reported directly to me, and I gave them equal footing with internal lawyers. They sat in internal management meetings and attended board meetings as observers."

There is wisdom in D'Alessandro's strategy. Many PR departments tend to get bogged down in the routine of issuing press releases, writing annual reports, and performing all the other necessary but mundane tasks associated with their roles. That type of PR department is at risk of missing big-picture trends on the horizon that may be far more important than quarterly earnings. Someone has to be looking into the future and doing it broadly, meaning across geographies and across industries. "You need someone who can read the radar before the ICBMs are launched," quips Marston.

One last aspect of the overall communications dilemma that bears mention is the international dimension. A growing number of companies, such as United Technologies and PepsiCo, are now earning more than half their revenues outside the United States. That means that how they position themselves in

China, India, Japan, and Germany, to cite just four major markets, is more important than ever to their bottom lines. In many of these markets, U.S. companies face a steady drumbeat of negativity because of opposition to the U.S. war in Iraq and because of concerns about aggressive American business practices. An added factor is that activist groups also operate across national borders, so they can pick at a company from multiple geographies. Technology compounds the challenge: a bad rumor that hits a blog in Thailand can pop up in the United States in a heartbeat.

CEOs understand that their brands are very important and that they should seek to emphasize the global nature of their products and services rather than their American origins. But very few companies have been able to deploy the international public affairs capabilities that are necessary to respond to the challenges of a globalizing economy. The vast majority of PR departments that I come into contact with are very U.S.-centric. If I approach a source from a company in Hong Kong or Japan, that source almost always has to get permission to speak to me from headquarters back in the States. It shouldn't be that ironclad. And if I were a Japanese or an Indian reporter, I would expect a major U.S. company to have decision makers on the ground in my market who could answer questions in my own language.

The roots of this problem are that CEOs have not expanded their PR operations as the composition of their sales and revenues has globalized. Many PR departments have a handful of U.S.-trained expatriates on the ground in key capitals, but not nearly enough. Some departments rely on public relations agencies that operate on a contractual basis, but again, that is no substitute for a full-fledged communications capability.

CEOs whose organizations are expanding internationally will ultimately have to decide whether to put sufficient resources into creating credible global PR capabilities and will have to wrestle with how to groom public relations people who have true international perspectives. Heretofore, most CEOs have not rotated many PR representatives from New York to Tokyo to Brussels to develop their skills and careers because that is expensive. CEOs do that for sales and technology and R&D because those functions are regarded as core to the company's success, but they don't think PR people are "worth it." But if communications is to be considered a core function, CEOs are going to need to move communications talent from Tokyo to New York, and vice versa, to create a cadre of communicators who can bridge very real cultural differences and project a common corporate message.

If the quality of the communications people is more important than the precise structure of their functions, the next corollary is that the culture in which they operate is crucial—and that culture is established by the CEO. Some of you allow the creation of vertical siloes in your organizations in which different departments and functions do not easily communicate or share information. That may have worked in one era, but in today's environment, it places the organization at risk.

A more open, inclusive style of communication, meaning that you communicate broadly and often, helps to defeat the internecine warfare between PR and IR departments, for example, or between internal and external PR advisers. It's painfully obvious that PR strategists ought to be able to see the information that IR departments are communicating to investors and help shape it. It's also obvious that IR people should welcome that, even if they report to the treasurer or CFO, not the SVP for communications. Creating the culture of cooperation is essential.

It's much the same in addressing the constant bickering between internal and external PR counsel. There's no question but that you ought to avail yourselves of the wisdom and insight that outside counselors can afford you. The key mistake is cutting out the internal PR people from those meetings and those conversations. They should be at the same table.

George Jamison of Spencer Stuart recalls how UTC CEO George David would summon his internal PR people for a meeting with external PR counsel. It was clear to Jamison and others that David was spurring them to greater levels of performance by showing them that they were engaged in a competition for his confidence. It was a kind of pressure tactic, and it worked. The best ideas were incorporated into the company's communications strategy. And David demonstrated that he was not "captive" to his internal advisers.

Once all these building blocks are in place, and communications skills have been inculcated into the whole organization's strategy and DNA, CEOs have a chance to go on the offensive in the complex battles swirling around them. And if ever there was a situation in which the old cliché, "To have a good defense, you gotta have a good offense" is true, today's corporate wars are it.

Go on the Offensive and
Shape the Message

One of the worst mistakes CEOs make is falling victim to what I call the "airline syndrome." Major American airlines (with the possible exceptions of Southwest and JetBlue) have conditioned themselves to respond to media inquiries only when they concern plane crashes, major disruptions of service, and other disasters. Too often, these responses are purely reactive and flat-footed. The airlines can't, or don't choose to, project broader, positive messages about what they are contributing to the American economy or what they are doing to promote understanding among peoples of the world. That's a mistake, and the regular drubbing they receive in the media reflects the vacuum.

But it is possible for CEOs to go on the offensive with their message. In fact, in today's climate it is essential. I would argue that there are two elements of projecting the message—one being personal relationships and the other the framing of the intellectual content of the message.

In the personal realm, chief executives should reach out and establish relationships with key news organizations and the reporters who cover their company. This is an incredibly powerful tool because so much journalism is personality-based.

The outreach effort may involve one dinner per month with three or four reporters or editors chosen by the SVP of communications. This effort can be modest in terms of how much of your time is spent. The emphasis in these meetings should be on getting to know reporters personally and to allowing them to get to know you as a person. Many senior leaders find that a difficult, awkward exercise, but it does not have to be, particularly if you are well prepared and if the ground rules of the conversations are clear. Typically, reporters will agree to quote "industry sources" or "sources close to the company" if you say anything interesting during these sessions.

Of course, it would be a disaster to expose a CEO whose personality is distant and arrogant to journalists in any setting. And CEOs have to be careful not to disclose any material financial information because of Regulation Fair Disclosure (Regulation FD). They also need to understand, or be counseled to understand, that there are certain subjects that need not be discussed. Whole Foods Market chief executive John Mackey made a terrible mistake, for example, by writing about the potential acquisition of Wild Oats Markets in an e-mail to his own board. He said it would represent "the elimination of a rival." That e-mail landed in the hands of the Federal Trade Commission, which sued to stop the acquisition.

But even if there are some constraints, the relationships created by personal contact can be crucial. And they can be particularly crucial in the event of a crisis—it makes a huge difference if a CEO has actually met the reporter on the other end of the telephone call. The worst-case scenario in public relations is for a crisis to erupt and for unknown reporters from major news organizations to start calling and asking, "What went wrong?"

That's a no-win situation. "You don't talk to the press when you *have* to," David D'Alessandro explains. "You talk to the press on an ongoing basis to form relationships, to give them a sense of trust, so that when you are in trouble, they will give you the benefit of the doubt. I'm not talking about whether you are stealing money or committing a criminal act. I am talking about when your company faces a crisis, you have people in the press in key publications who say, 'I have met the CEO on a number of occasions. I know he is not lying. He may have been ill-advised. But his mea culpa counts.'"

D'Alessandro says he spent time with journalists he absolutely loathed, but he felt compelled to make the effort. The penalty for not developing those relationships was abundantly clear. "When you are arrogant and believe that the rules of engagement do not apply to you, you will have no friends," he adds. "You will inevitably get lit up"—he means being on the receiving end of negative publicity.

By using the CEO to open doors, top public relations professionals can then also capture relationships with journalists they might not otherwise have been able to meet. Journalists often resist quasi-social entreaties from PR people; not so when the CEO is involved. All this assists in the process of building equity and trust, which are highly elusive in the relationship between a company and the press—but not impossible.

I recall covering Ford's massive recall of vehicles equipped with Firestone tires in the late 1990s. In preparing a story under deadline pressures for *U.S. News & World Report,* I had to make a basic gut-level evaluation of whether I thought Ford was telling the truth. I had interviewed Ford CEO Jacques Nasser and thought I understood his values and strategy. And I had a liking for New York–based Ford PR man Tom Rhodes, who spent time with reporters at events

one is fired or legal action is taken. Competition among various news organizations can fan the flames of these crusades. It is always possible that a fatigue factor will set in and the media's attention will be distracted, but that cannot be controlled by any company.

So at the highest level, you should be able to articulate how what your company does is positive for society or some portion thereof. The days of simply allowing your financial results to serve as the dominant message are fast vanishing. This high-level message should mesh with the strategic vision for the company as a whole and have a direct but subtle connection with business goals. "The best CEOs, those who truly lead, make statements and decisions based on values and principles that reflect what they genuinely believe in," says Kathy Bloomgarden, CEO of New York–based public relations firm, Ruder Finn.

The broad statement of mission or purpose should be accompanied by other, more tangible goals, such as penetrating certain markets or geographies. Financial results are a part of the message, but just a part. This architecture of messages must be created with the CEO's personal involvement because it is central to how he or she intends to run the business. Different levels of management, and indeed all employees, need to buy in. It is not an exercise in showmanship. "In terms of the 'architecture' of the message, it's really important to build an aligned team, have engaged leadership at many levels and involve employees throughout the organization in the rollout of a distinct mission and vision for the company," says Bloomgarden.

One of the best examples of a CEO with a winning message architecture is William C. Weldon, of Johnson & Johnson. The cover of the company's most recent annual report says simply: "Johnson & Johnson: Our passion transforms." Then Weldon's letter to shareholders begins: "Improving the health and well-being of people around the world is a vital and important business. It is perhaps the world's most meaningful business and, for that reason, attracts exceptional people who are capable, skilled, and possess a genuine passion for making a difference in people's lives."

It is brilliant positioning. Although it might be easy to dismiss as rhetoric, the evidence is that J&J employees believe it—and that the media believe it. J&J does not exactly get a free ride from the media—after all, it was the company that suffered the Tylenol disaster. But a news organization that went after J&J today would have to overcome the accumulation of goodwill that Weldon and his predecessors have generated. The onus of deciding whether to attack J&J for some perceived wrongdoing would be heavier than if the same reporter wanted to criticize Halliburton, to cite an extreme example.

Of course, CEOs cannot completely control their message. One problem can be leaks. It's hard to define what a leak is in today's environment when board members, managers, and employees may all be blogging or engaging in extensive external e-mail communications. If the message they project is consistent with what top management desires, that is seen as positive reinforcement. But if it runs counter to the CEO's message, as was the case at Hewlett-Packard, then it is considered leaking.

There's precious little that you can do to stop leaks. The effort by HP chairwoman Patricia Dunn to plug the leaks at her company backfired badly. Wal-Mart's internal risk control group also imploded, revealing unsavory monitoring of communications.

In my experience, the problem of leaking is too deep to be resolved through traditional PR means or internal investigations. The existence of leaks means that there is deep dysfunction in the organization and that key players are at odds with the strategy and direction charted by top management. Fixing that requires deep internal deliberations, not band-aid fixes.

So it is possible, and indeed imperative, for CEOs to think about how to frame their messages. Many executives I've met over the years have felt they have a compelling message, but those messages often were too self-interested and did not resonate in the context of the public debate. They almost always fell flat. The key is to first understand the public dialogue and to position the corporate message in it, rather than the other way around. That requires extensive reading, listening, and viewing to get a sense of the public zeitgeist. The best CEOs have an intuitive knowledge of how to do that; others rely on their communications counselors.

One issue that CEOs have largely failed to frame properly is their own compensation, which has emerged as one of the hottest issues uniting disparate shareholder activist groups. Of course, there are some cases where CEOs have reaped huge personal gains at a time when their companies were suffering layoffs or losing money. That's indefensible. But even CEOs who are creating huge wealth for shareholders and employees, while innovating and satisfying customer demands around the world, have difficulty explaining that there is a connection between broader corporate performance and their own compensation. The critics have been able to define the field of battle by comparing a CEO's compensation to the performance of the company's shares. That linkage was firmly established in media coverage of Robert Nardelli's pay and also that of Verizon's Ivan Seidenberg.

activist groups are doing, but there are limits on just how much those efforts can accomplish.

Ultimately, you need to decide which activist groups your company can work with and engage in serious dialogue. Many external groups such as the Christian Brothers or Environmental Defense are far more interested in starting substantive discussions with a company than in embarrassing it publicly. Each of this multitude of groups has a different reputation and track record. After deciding which ones to engage with, CEOs and their companies can then decide to "do something big," in the words of Richard Edelman, to defuse the criticism. Not all activist groups or NGOs can be negotiated with, because some of their demands are inherently unreasonable. But if you are selective and agile in working with a handful of external advocacy groups, the net effect will be that no broad coalition will be formed. The Wal-Mart syndrome will be avoided.

The first step is early detection. PR staffs should be doing risk assessments to see what groups are considering targeting the company, and that information needs to be in the CEO's hands—early. "The problem is that CEOs wait until someone is coming at them," says Kathy Bloomgarden of Ruder Finn. "That's the wrong approach today. You know you're going to have to engage with NGOs and other activist third parties. If you wait, you're really on the defensive. Then it is seen as the company versus whatever the group is demanding." The sense of confrontation eggs on media coverage because NGOs are the most trusted organizations in the world, according to the Edelman study on public perception. The story becomes the evil CEO fighting the white knights.

It's therefore a mistake to be perceived as fighting an NGO. "CEOs need to realize they need to be engaged with the NGO community," maintains Bloomgarden. "Traditionally, that was delegated fairly [low] in the ranks, if at all." The approach to these groups should be consistent and coordinated, she says, adding, "Of course, there can be very emotional disagreements. But some bridges can be established."

Many CEOs appear to think that even meeting with an activist group exposes them to negative publicity or legal risks. But Leslie Gaines-Ross of Weber Shandwick disagrees. "It's the companies that don't listen or don't meet with these coalitions that really run a risk," she says. "You don't run a risk by meeting with critics and listening to what they have to say. If you don't make the time and don't listen and make it clear that you don't want an outside perspective, you run a much greater risk."

Gaines-Ross says groups such as Greenpeace and Amnesty International want to talk to CEOs and

from Costa Rica are part of Starbucks's effort to show that it is sensitive to the financial needs of Latin American farmers. "Howard Shultz is a fantastic advocate," says Richard Edelman. "It's a virtuous circle. It's good for all parties. It's good for farmers. It's good for consumers."

Oxfam also targeted the company for the way it markets Ethiopian coffee under certain Ethiopian brand names. Oxfam demanded that Starbucks sign a licensing agreement for use of regional Ethiopian coffee names. Investors raised the issue at the company's annual shareholder meeting in March and the company agreed to do so.

Starbucks clearly has learned to project a positive environmental image that seems to anesthetize it to protest. For example, it recently ran full-page ads in newspapers proclaiming, "You Can Change the World." The ads were timed to help celebrate Earth Day on April 22, 2007. "In the pursuit of progress, humans have brought about real change to the planet's climate, and this change, left unchecked, will cause ecological and societal disruption on a grand scale," they proclaimed. The ads then proceeded to outline how Starbucks tries to contribute to environmental leadership by, among other things, the way it sources its coffee beans. A company that was once targeted for exploitation is now urging progress on global warming! By wrapping itself in eco-friendliness, Starbucks has largely defused Oxfam's campaign.

Here are other examples of how CEOs have responded to critics with campaigns that combine elements of public relations and business strategy:

- Unilever partnered with the World Wildlife Fund in 1997 to create the independent, non-profit Marine Stewardship Council, which is aimed at reducing overfishing around the world. The council certifies that certain fisheries engage in environmentally sustainable fishing practices and allows them to affix a blue "ecolabel" to their products. Unilever, which makes food products in addition to home care and personal care products, changed its business practices, but did so in a way that has allowed it to continue to make money over the past decade.

- Coca Cola's Neville Isdell supports the Global Water Challenge, an initiative of the United Nations Foundation and the Better World Fund. The purpose of this partnership is to provide safe drinking water, sanitation, and hygiene education around the world. It's in Coke's self-interest, in part, because the company depends on having access to safe water to create its beverages.

and expects companies to build a better society," says Gaines-Ross, whose forthcoming book is entitled *Corporate Reputation: Twelve Steps to Safeguarding and Recovering Reputations*.

The broad rubric that activist groups are pursuing is "sustainability," and that touches on both environmental and human aspects, such as child labor, fair wages, and education. "Some of the research that we've done shows that companies that have better reputations in the sustainability area are able to recover their reputations faster," says Gaines-Ross. "It can't prevent you from losing your reputation but it can help you recover. If you look at BP, despite all the problems they're experiencing, they could be at a real low if they didn't have a real, global climate change initiative."

In the cases where a company is successful in defusing an external assault, one key seems to be that public relations and corporate social responsibility are built into the business strategy. This marks a clear evolution for both of these functions, which often have been marginalized inside companies. Author and professor Michael Porter, in a widely noted *Harvard Business Review* article published late last year, argued that companies will increasingly integrate CSR, in particular, into their business goals and objectives. Porter argued that CEOs should not view the social demands being placed on them as being fundamentally at odds with the profit imperative. Business shouldn't be pitted against society because the two are interdependent. Instead, companies such as Whole Foods and Toyota (think hybrids) integrate a social responsibility consideration into how they design and market their products, which has had a positive impact on their bottom lines. So no one is suggesting that you should not be pursuing profits; it merely seems that you must do so in a slightly more sophisticated way.

So what can a CEO do in the face of an intractable external foe that is relying extensively on media coverage? There's a debate among PR experts on whether CEOs can create coalitions of employees, suppliers, customers, and others to counterattack. Richard Edelman says employees can be particularly effective. "Look how successful Starbucks has been with what I call an 'inside-out' strategy of talking to the baristas, the people who make the coffee, as if they are as important as the investors . . . The baristas know all about ethical-sourced coffee. An informed employee is your best ally."

The broader lesson, in his view, is this: "What this puts an exclamation point on is that employee communications, which was always at the back of the line, has to move to the front of the line. Your employees have to become your advocate."

Others aren't so sure about the effectiveness of internal coalitions. Kathy Bloomgarden says they may be effective in blogging or creating flows of information that help counteract external accusations, but it ultimately will create a kind of "chaos" if employees are distracted from doing their jobs. And Dick Martin says CEOs have to be careful about trying to create their own grassroots movements because they will be perceived as "Astroturf," meaning artificial.

The broader point on which the experts agree is that CEOs cannot remain in their bunkers while various shareholder activists or NGOs contemplate changing the way the company does business. If CEOs engage, they can work with selected groups and still achieve their business goals, perhaps even enhance their business performance. In so doing, they can prevent the emergence of broad-based coalitions—because single-cause activist groups, if isolated, find it much more difficult to get traction in the marketplace of ideas.

Embrace the New Media

When *New York Times* columnist Thomas Friedman attacked General Motors in a column in May 2006, he used surprisingly strident language. He wrote that GM was "more dangerous to America's future" than any other company and was "like a crack dealer" addicting helpless Americans to sport utility vehicles. General Motors didn't appreciate the comments and asked the newspaper to print its response. But the editors declined. So GM documented their refusal and then went on the attack—on the company's blog, called GM Fastlane (http://fastlane.gmblogs.com).

It is instructive that even a company long known as a lumbering giant is now resorting to electronic combat. Senior communications executive Steve Harris used equally strident language in a posting entitled "Hyperbole and Defamation in the *New York Times*." "These weren't the rantings of some obscure, clueless blogger," Harris wrote. "These were the thoughts of Thomas Friedman, author and influential columnist, on the op/ed page of the *New York Times*. Mr. Fried-man is not normally known for such shrill hyper-bole." Friedman responded to GM in a subsequent print column.

The fact that two major American institutions would carry out a battle of ideas at least partly online is instructive. Electronic forms of communication have not replaced the printed word, but clearly they are com-peting as never before. Mainstream news organizations, many of them struggling to find viable economic models, are shedding reporters, editors, and produc-ers, while shifting other resources to online sites.

Partly because established news organizations have stripped themselves of much talent, for the first time the so-called "gatekeepers" of professional journal-ism are responding to their less trained and less tested electronic brethren at places like BuzzMachine and Matt Drudge's Drudge Report. Stories originating online are forcing their way into print rather than the other way around. "For the first time in my career, I can see how stories start out on blogs and then three or four days later, they start showing up in the *Times* or the *Wall Street Journal*," says James Horton of Robert Marston and Associates, who has maintained the site www.online-pr.com for ten years. Adds Leslie Gaines-Ross: "They're fighting over who's going to be the ultimate authority. That's the battle we're going to see over the next five years. It's over who really owns the news."

There are at least four related technologies helping to increase the prominence of electronic communications:

- **Blogs:** Anyone can start one and they are essentially free. Altogether, 70 million blogs have been set up, but March 2007 data from blog search service Technorati shows that only 15.5 million bloggers updated their sites during the past three months. That suggests there are that many active blogs. The vast majority of blog content is undisciplined and unfocused, but enough blogs have sufficiently compelling content that they are clearly a force to be reckoned with. "There's almost a sense that the blogs are out there only to focus on wrongdoing, to stir up rumors and myths," says Leslie Gaines-Ross. "Blogs can really ruin the reputations of CEOs if they reveal something."

- **The ease of creation of new Web sites:** Because they are so cheap and the software now is so widely available and accessible, Web sites that unite various opponents can be created by critics. Some, like Untied.com, exist purely as a collection point for complaints about a company, in this case United Airlines. Others like Wal-Mart Watch are the focal points for wide-ranging grassroots activism. Employee Web sites also spring up and can be quite powerful, as in the case of starbucksgossip .com (the site proclaims that it is "monitoring America's favorite drug dealer").

- **Social sites:** The growth of MySpace, Facebook, and YouTube have caught most established companies by surprise. YouTube, in particular, has become important to companies because mostly young people post videos of favorite products or, more ominously, videos criticizing products or the companies that make them. For example, when JetBlue's flights were badly delayed in February 2007 because of winter weather, enterprising young travelers took videos of themselves stuck at airports and posted them on YouTube. The ubiquitous nature of video cameras and wireless laptop computers allows that kind of guerrilla communications.

- **Search engines:** These have helped revolutionize the world of communications. Individuals use Google or Yahoo! to search for information, and those searches obviously produce lists of Web sites. If all the Web sites on the critical first two pages of the search are negative about your company's products or you personally, that can be devastating.

All this has scary implications for today's CEOs, nearly all of whom built their careers long before the Internet reached its current level of sophistication. Your major fears now are loss of control over the flow of information and over your brand names. "CEOs and very senior people are just facing the facts that anything you do internally might as well be external," says Gaines-Ross. "There is no seam anymore, or boundary, between internal and external. We see that at Wal-Mart and everywhere. An employee simply spills the beans on what's happening. Companies are living in glass houses." Wal-Mart CEO Lee Scott did make some internal e-mail comments that were leaked to the press. For would-be leakers, it's as simple as hitting the "forward" button on their e-mail.

The fact that so much internal information may find its way to external audiences carries major implications for your ability to control sensitive information about technology or financial performance. There are very strict rules in place, thanks to Regulation FD, that companies cannot disclose financial information to one audience and not all investors at the same time. The climate of shareholder litigation also imposes a layer of caution. If you or one of your key executives were to make a statement that a lawyer, one year or five years later, was able to document as misleading, the potential for class action lawsuits would be high. CEOs are just now waking up to the implications of this issue—how can companies adhere to the new standards of "accountability" yet still shield core strategic and financial information from unwanted scrutiny?

Another implication of the democratization of communications is that brands and reputations are exposed as never before. Simon McDermott, cofounder and chief executive of Attentio, a Brussels-based Internet monitoring company, was quoted in the *Financial Times* as saying: "Brands are completely exposed in social media. It's inevitable that people are going to talk about you, for good or ill, and they may well have a propensity to write some pretty negative stuff."[7]

Many of you, probably most, have not even begun to respond to these technological developments. "The CEOs of the largest fifty companies in the world are practically hiding under their desks in terror about Internet rumors," crisis manager Eric Dezenhall told *BusinessWeek*. "Millions of dollars of labor are being spent discussing whether or not you should respond to the Web."[8]

What, then, must be done? As in dealing with outside activist groups, getting early alerts about online activity around the world is essential. This means watching blogs and social sites, and being sensitive to "buzz." "It's important to detect the early warning signs," says Gaines-Ross. "Look at the obesity issue. If someone had really been tracking the fact that people themselves were being blamed for being obese, they would have seen that the marketers of the products were starting to get blamed for how fat people are. The food companies should have been more alert that they were going to get the blame."

Another example was Sony and its defective batteries. "Exploding laptops were all over the Internet," Gaines-Ross says. "Maybe with better intelligence, Sony would have seen it coming."

Who should be doing the monitoring? It seems obvious that you should build some capabilities in your own PR departments, which almost certainly means hiring young people who will spend hours surfing the Web. They can use tools such as technorati .com, which is essentially a search engine for blogs. The user enters the subject or name and can adjust the search for three variables—what range of blogs should be searched; whether blogs with great authority or little authority should be searched; and which languages should be searched. There are also contact monitoring services that can keep an eye on what is being said such as http://www.customscoop.com and http://www.cymfony.com/.

Building an internal Internet capability may not be enough, however. External PR firms are zeroing in on this area of specialization and offer certain advantages, says Kathy Bloomgarden, whose own firm is competing for such business. "In terms of managing the whole online space, some companies do have in-house teams but the technology is changing so much that it's better to have outside input," she argues.

Her firm has an interactive department of seventy people. One of the roles of that group is to conduct focus groups with high school and college students to learn about how they are using their computers. "That's where the innovation is coming from and the new habits," she says. "You need to have a focus group that's outside the corporate setting."

Other companies provide slightly different offerings. Nielsen Media Research will survey the online world and report back to a company. Another useful tool is ReputationDefender.com, which will search for negative information about a company on the Net and then try to bump up positive articles in the search engine rankings so that a more balanced portrait of a company emerges. It tells the story of one CEO who watched a negative story about his company drop from the first page of his Google hits to the third page. Another outside vendor with an interesting twist is BuzzLogic, which uses algorithms to analyze which bloggers and social media are driving online gabfests. It's useful to know who the most influential commentators actually are.

In the final analysis, the skills and communications style of a CEO's Internet team is more important than the precise organizational structure. The team has to be smart enough to know which Internet-based reports are "viral," meaning that they stand a good chance of spreading to other online outlets or into the established media. And it has to be mature enough to recognize which online phenomena should be communicated to the CEO and top management—and which postings and sites are likely to get lost in the electronic clutter.

To blog or not to blog is another key question. Not everyone can be Jonathan Schwartz, CEO of Sun Microsystems, who maintains an extensive blog. Microsoft's top brass isn't blogging externally, but the company has five thousand employee bloggers. Some companies like Dell have appointed "chief bloggers." Blogging "makes sense for some companies, but not for all," says Bloomgarden. "You have to maintain it. You have to have enough material to make it interesting. It's difficult to do that well."

Whatever precise mix of online communications a company uses, the emerging principles seem to include these: a company must respond in kind, meaning using the same kind of media that a critic has used (One exception may be that Dell finally neutralized a highly critical "Dell Hell" blogger by meeting with him personally and hearing his concerns.) Further, you must respond in a way that integrates various media channels, such as online, print, and television. The old days of just putting out a press release are long gone.

Here are recent examples of how companies have used new media tools:

- Wal-Mart produced its own movie to counteract an anti-Wal-Mart video that was posted on YouTube. It also created a blog to counteract Wal-Mart Watch and Wake-Up Wal-Mart, the two labor-backed opposition groups. (However, Wal-Mart got nailed when an external PR firm created a phony blog around a family visiting Wal-Marts across the country.)

- David Neeleman at JetBlue wrote an e-mail of apology to every single customer affected by the extensive flight delays in February. And he put a videotaped apology on YouTube, saying, "It won't happen again." Then he appeared on David Letterman's late-night television show, and that segment was also placed on YouTube. PR pros point to this episode as a particularly good example of how a CEO personally led a communications effort and how his company integrated a variety of media vehicles to make the CEO a more effective communicator.

• Robert Nardelli's successor at Home Depot, Francis S. Blake, found himself in a tough position after *MSN Money* columnist Scott Burns accused the company of being a "consistent abuser" of customers' time because of bad in-store service. Within hours, the *MSN Money* Web site received ten thousand angry e-mails and four thousand postings. It was the biggest response in *MSN Money*'s history. Blake could have ignored the episode, but he wisely chose to write a repentant online letter, promising to increase staffing in stores. Home Depot's own employees took note and applauded his efforts on an unofficial employee site called the Orange Blood Bank.

Sometimes a little humor helps. One revealing case is how Coca-Cola responded to two young people in lab coats who created volcanic Coke bottles. They dropped packages of Mentos candy into two-liter Diet Coke bottles, causing the drink to shoot violently out of the bottle and into the air. Amateur videographers captured the scene and posted it on YouTube and other Web video sites.

The traditional corporate response would have been one of deep concern. Stern lawyers might have called the families involved and threatened YouTube with lawsuits for violating Coke's brand name. But instead, CEO Isdell told a press conference that the videos were "great." "I love them," he said. "We're a fun brand." He also said it was "one of our best campaigns last year." So, confronted by seeming lack of control over how his brand was being presented, Isdell very cleverly got on the bandwagon and rode it. In the Internet world, you cannot control messages, but you can learn how to respond in the right spirit.

The key is to create what Bloomgarden calls "balance" in the online debate. This is an important concept. Negative voices can't be eliminated but they can be put in a new context. "In a world where everybody has a voice, other constituencies should be expressing their point of view in order to balance the dialogue," she says. "If you do a search and only find things that the critics have put out, there's no balance. There needs to be real information so that people can make their own judgments."

Of course, the Holy Grail is discovering how to go on the offensive on the Internet, and this is an area of intense activity at the moment. CEOs are beginning to realize that they can use the Internet to identify the right groups of customers and to engage them in communication. Boston-based Forrester Research says companies are pouring resources into this quest because they realize it is much more selective than other forms of mass media. More intimate conversations can be achieved. And a survey of U.S. brand marketers carried out by online analysts Jupiter-Research found that almost half were planning to advertise on the social media networking sites such as MySpace, Bebo, and Facebook this year.

The key is that millions of Americans are hungry for information, and they're turning to searches on the Internet and other online resources to get it. "The way to use the online community is to reach out to people," says Bloomgarden. "It can be better than advertising on TV, which reaches a huge broad community. If you make a food product for dieters, for example, you can reach people in a very targeted way. You can find exactly the people you want to be communicating with." Companies that do this well may be able gain insight into product development, consumer needs, and strategic opportunities.

One problem area is that marketers, unlike the smartest PR people, are reluctant to approach bloggers. Marketers are too sales-oriented and don't understand that if they supply the right information, bloggers will be mature enough to decide whether they like a product or not. "The approach one uses is important, especially if a blogger expresses unhappiness with a brand," says James Horton. "Customer service should respond with an invitation to talk to the company and to explain the problem so the company can resolve it." This is the art of turning negatives into positives.

As with so many other aspects of the PR wars, being on the defensive is not much fun nor is it very effective. It is far better to learn how to project and reach out. So while justifiably concerned about some aspects of what the Internet is doing to flows of information and brand names, you should attempt to take advantage of the opportunities that it offers. The Internet is not the enemy.

Conclusion:
Creating Organizations
That Communicate

For too long, American CEOs have concluded that it is impossible to engage with the media in any meaningful way. You have assumed that the media will always be a negative factor in how you conduct your business. You have concluded that the media are unfair and prejudiced against you. Reflecting that view, most of you have engaged in a policy of benign neglect toward the media.

But that strategy no longer works. Something in the air has changed. The terms "inflection point" and "paradigm shift" have been overused and therefore rendered meaningless, but as I have argued that there appear to be two major factors that have transformed the climate in which you operate:(1) the proliferation and growing power of external activist groups and their demands that CEOs articulate a vision that goes beyond earnings per share, and (2) the increasing use of Internet-based communication technologies. Companies' rapidly growing global revenues, and an attendant need to project coherent messages in multiple markets, is yet another major factor.

Because CEOs are the ultimate pragmatists, you should recognize that a different operating climate requires a different business model in which sensitivity to communications in the broadest sense is built into business strategy and elevated in the management structure of your company.

As with many issues in the corporate world, fixing a problem requires starting at the top—with the board. Aside from lacking members with communications or journalistic backgrounds, the vast majority of boards do not discuss communications or reputational risk on a regular basis. That's odd, given that, in the post-Sarbanes-Oxley era, risk management has arguably become the board's number-one function. Boards are consumed with trying to identify risks and to mitigate them by making sure management is responding appropriately. Now boards will also have to engage on issues of perception and reputation, the experts argue. "Unless the board is asleep at the switch, they have to do it," says Robert Dilenschneider, founder and chairman of New York–based communications firm The Dilenschneider Group. "The problem that most boards face is that they don't have adequate internal sources in the company to really gauge the company's reputation . . . They are not getting the research and they're not getting the feedback on how all these different audiences feel about the company. They're not asking themselves, 'What are our options? How should we be consulting with the CEO? What direction should we be offering to the communications team?'"

In his view, communications issues ought to be on the agenda for every board meeting. "It should be more than a report about something that already happened," says Dilenschneider, author most recently of *Power and Influence: The Rules Have Changed.*[9] "It should be a forward-looking statement about what's going to happen. It should take into account the reputation of the company, but more importantly the environment and climate that the company's going to have to operate in."

It once would have been heresy to suggest that boards should develop a separate communications ability apart from management. But the growing number of assaults and pressures on boards almost certainly means that at least in some situations, boards are going to have to find a collective voice separate from management's. "Given the hostile business environment, boards will need to develop trained spokes-persons to deal with outside critics, including the media," says Robert Marston. "The old concept of 'what happens in the boardroom stays in the board-room' is no longer viable. ISS and CalPERS and other institutional investors are now demanding answers from companies and are calling on board members to explain and change what they consider to be fla-grant behavior and poor management practices." In Marston's view, boards can no longer "hide behind company management or their lawyers. They must face the music directly and deal with their critics pro-fessionally or the end game will be lost."

Change is also required at the CEO level. You need to recognize that your job definitions have changed. "Facing the new challenges, the CEO has to step up his commitment to communications, to be more ac-cessible, more regularly and more honestly," says Kathy Bloomgarden. "The role of the CEO has changed and the portfolio of responsibilities has changed. You have to look at what your goals are, look at the repu-tation of the company and instill values in the com-pany. You can't worry only about the performance of the numbers." Dilenschneider puts it in starker terms: "Any CEO in today's environment who does not know how to deal with a whole raft of constituencies, which a CEO didn't even touch on ten years ago, is headed for failure."

One underlying explanation is that, in the horizontal and more democratic communications environment that has been created, CEOs have a much greater symbolic value than ever before. Your personalities and communications styles are coming under greater scrutiny. A majority of CEOs who hang back and hide in the shadows will come to regret it; other CEOs who learn how to exploit the power of new external partners and who learn how to use new communications tools and channels will be able to lead in a new and even more dynamic way.

The way not to lose control over how a company is perceived by multiple constituencies is to be actively engaged in shaping the messages that are projected to them. These issues of reputation and communications strategy ought to be on the agenda when top management teams meet, just as when boards meet. And the top communications professional ought to be at the table.

At the organizational level, CEOs need to realize that public relations and related functions are core to business strategy and business success. For too many years, PR people have existed in a kind of ghetto—

they can rise up the ranks in communications but they have no chance of moving into business lines and they have little chance of moving up to top leadership positions.

From a CEO's perspective, the first step in correcting the problem is spending as much time and money finding talent for the communications function as for R&D or manufacturing or finance. "What it means is getting the smartest people, the smartest strategists you possibly can find, and putting them in the communications function," says Dilenschneider. "Too often, you've just got a bag carrier who takes orders. The CEO or somebody hands them a press release and says, 'Put this out.'"

That's highly dysfunctional. "It ought to work the other way," Dilenschneider argues. "The communications person ought to go to the board or the CEO and say, 'Here's what we need to put out and here's why. I see a storm cloud coming. Or I see this opportunity on the horizon.' Too few communications people do that."

To truly break down the PR ghetto, you should invest in communication skills training for all high-potential managers who have a shot at one day becoming CEOs themselves. That means the subject should be built into executive development programs. And it's not outside the realm of reason to argue that some percentage of the compensation of key executives ought to be based on their ability to communicate. If it can be measured, it can be rewarded, as the old expression goes.

For any of that to happen, the HR function would have to be sensitive to public relations and communications issues, which it is not today. A smart CEO might move a handful of PR people into HR, and vice versa, for one- or two-year assignments. If HR departments are going to be involved in recommending board candidates and grooming future CEOs, they must have some sense of the skills and values that are desirable.

Practitioners of public relations, both inside companies and outside, also need to recognize that their profession is undergoing a wrenching change. In some senses, the very definition of "public relations" has changed. "In the old days, it was very narrowly focused on media relations," says Marston. "But now the job hinges on integrating many different communications functions, including social responsibility, and projecting a message to a much more complex array of constituencies. And all that has to be deeply connected to the CEO's business objectives. PR people have to be business partners like never before."

In sum, the right skills and values should be inculcated from the board level to the CEO and throughout the company. The entire organization needs to be able to project a sense of strategic mission. You and your company need to anticipate what external groups are saying about you. The organization should be technologically savvy in monitoring the Internet and should be responding and anticipating in multiple languages twenty-four hours a day around the world.

Crises cannot be entirely avoided, but smart organizations will see many of them coming and anticipate them. When a crisis does truly erupt as a complete surprise, the CEO who has built up goodwill and a kind of intangible equity in the marketplace will be able to recover more quickly than one who has not invested the time or money.

CEOs who take the PR challenge seriously and build the right teams and the right messages can be hugely effective in shaping media perceptions. The media are not a hostile monolith. They are, in fact, quite malleable, particularly in view of the rise of so many online voices. The media most decidedly cannot be controlled, but they can be harnessed to help CEOs communicate with disparate constituencies.

The reality is almost 180 degrees in the opposite direction of what many of you believe. You do have real communications power, if you choose to use it. CEOs can, in fact, use the media to enhance their global businesses and to spotlight their companies' contributions to the markets they serve. It is not inevitable that you become losers in the media wars.

Here are some practical questions for you to consider and possible courses of action:

- Which audiences do you really care about? It's obvious that you care about Wall Street and your bankers, but other audiences include customers, suppliers, employees, governments, shareholders, and so forth. Where is your company's image strongest, and where does it need help? It's possible that you have an excellent reputation with the financial community but an awful one with employees. That's not healthy or balanced. Your goal is to have a positive image with every constituency.

- What does your board think about your company's image among these different constituencies? That would be a useful conversation, probably best held informally on the night before a board meeting. Open up the discussion. Let the ideas flow. This will allow you to assess which board members actually understand this set of issues. If no one rises to the challenge, you need to work with the nominating committee to bring in at least one director who understands issues of reputation and communications.

- Build the issue of image and reputation into your dialogue with the different constituencies when you travel. Rather than simply staging town hall meetings with employees to share your vision of the future, create environments in which people can speak to you with a measure of candor. GM CEO Rick Wagoner, for example, holds "diagonal" meetings with employees, meaning he cuts through the organization to pluck people from different levels. They are able to speak to him without their managers present.

- Once you know how your board perceives these issues and you have gathered some input from key constituencies, it may be time for a candid conversation with your top internal communications people, with or without external PR counsel present. What I would be looking for here is whether your communications people have a solid understanding of just where the company stands with its external and internal audiences. If they sugarcoat the truth, you either need to readjust their attitude or bring in a new team. Too many PR people are inclined to tell you what they think you want to hear. That's crippling. You want people who will say things that might make you a bit uncomfortable. You want people you can trust and treat as partners.

- Do some introspection as well. How much of your time is devoted to communication? Are you an effective speaker? If not, get some media coaching. Are you communicating a message, or messsages, that can provide a rallying point for your employees? Do you communicate about a theme or message that you really believe in? There's almost no way to fake it. If you give a speech about something you don't really believe in, everyone will know it. Organizations have finely tuned antennae; they know when they are receiving an authentic message as opposed to one that isn't.

This is just a quick checklist, but I'd suggest that it is possible for any CEO to spend a modest amount of time and money and improve the way your company is perceived. The rate of return on that investment could be huge.

Notes

1. Unless otherwise attributed, quotations are from interviews conducted by the author between [month, year] and [month, year]. All parties have given permission to be quoted in this book.

2. http://www.comptroller.nyc.gov/press/2007_releases/pr07-04-040.shtm

3. Michael Barbaro and Steven Greenhouse, "Wal-Mart Chief Writes off New York," *New York Times,* March 28, 2007.

4. Alan Murray, *The Wall Street Journal,* "How Countrywide CEO Wins Amid Mortgage Mayhem," March 7, 2007.

5. Siobhan Hughes and Kaja Whitehouse, "Labor Fights Verizon Board Over CEO's Compensation," *The Wall Street Journal,* April 5, 2007.

6. http://www3.weforum.org/en/events/AnnualMeeting2007/IssuesinDepth/TheCoca-ColaCompany/index.html

7. Stefan Stern, "Master New Technology or Be Ruled by the Unruly Mob," *Financial Times* online (www.ft.com), Apr 23, 2007.

8. "Web Attack: Nastiness Online Can Erupt and Go Global Overnight, and 'No Comment' Doesn't Cut It Anymore. Here's How to Cope," *BusinessWeek* online (www.businessweek.com), April 16, 2007.

About the Author

William J. Holstein is an award-winning editor, author, and journalist who writes about topics affecting chief executive officers and boards of directors. Currently, he is a columnist for the *New York Times* business section; he also contributes to *Barron's*, *Corporate Board Member*, *Fortune*, *Dealmaker*, *Strategy & Business*, and reviews cars for *Portfolio* magazine. He has spent thirty years in the writing world specializing in global business issues and his previous books include *The Japanese Power Game* and *Rags to Riches* (coauthored with Richard T. Farmer). His other areas of interest include innovation, competitiveness, and governance.